JN192877

Lina Bo Bardi

Casa de Vidro

Residential Masterpieces 22
Lina Bo Bardi
Casa de Vidro

Text and edited by Yoshio Futagawa
Photographed by Yukio Futagawa
Art direction: Gan Hosoya

Printed and bound in Japan

ISBN 978-4-87140-647-5 C1352

Lina Bo Bardi

Casa de Vidro

São Paulo, Brazil, 1950-51

Text by Yoshio Futagawa

Photographed by Yukio Futagawa

世界現代住宅全集22

リナ・ボ・バルディ
ガラスの家
サンパウロ，ブラジル　1950-51

文・編集：二川由夫

企画・撮影：二川幸夫

大きな器としての建築――二川由夫
Architecture as a Large Vessel *by Yoshio Futagawa*

第二次大戦後，ブラジル建築は世界的な注目を集めることとなったが，この国の建築界を未来に向けて大きく動かすことになった功労者はルシオ・コスタ，オスカー・ニーマイヤーやヴィラノヴァ・アルチガスら，ヨーロッパ・モダニズムに学んだブラジル人建築家たちだけではない。戦後イタリアからやってきた一人の女性建築家／デザイナー，リナ・ボ・バルディもまた重要な役割を果たしたことは，昨今の彼女についての様々な言及や展覧会などでも明らかなことである。彼女はモダニズムの理論やヨーロッパ建築の歴史的伝統の系譜などといった建築の原理的な様式，理論や思想をブラジルに持ち込んだのではなく，むしろアカデミズムの堅苦しさから解放して，建築の領域を拡大するようなものであった。彼女は自由で大らかに社会や日常生活を彩る美しさの発見の仕方，それらの育て方をブラジルにもたらした。彼女が携えた新しい文化や社会の精神は，ブラジルの，コロニアル時代以前から近現代を横断しそれらの時代毎に散りばめられた，この大地に生まれる独特な美の世界を現代の表舞台に呼び出し，現在進行形の建築／デザインをブラジル固有の，フュージョンし自由で豊かな様相に仕立て上げたのである。

リナ・ボ・バルディはイタリア，ローマに生まれた。彼女はローマ大学建築学部を卒業後，ミラノに居を移し，建築家としてのキャリアをスタートさせた。しかし，当時，戦争のため設計依頼は少なく，建築以外の仕事をこなし

ていくことになる。雑誌『ドムス』の初代編集長で建築家／デザイナーであるジオ・ポンティと協働して雑誌を手がけたり，雑誌や新聞のために挿絵を描いたりした。戦後，『ドムス』の編集長を1年余り勤めた後，ローマに戻り，美術評論家／ジャーナリストのピエトロ・マリア・バルディと結婚する。

この夫婦は戦争の影響で停滞していたイタリアを後にし，新天地ブラジルに未来を獲得することになる。リナはまずリオ・デ・ジャネイロでコミッションを得て，夫ピエトロは「サンパウロ美術館（MASP）」(1957-68年)の設立，運営を任されることになり，夫婦はサンパウロに移住する。結局二人は終生この地で暮らすことになった。

「カーザ・デ・ヴィドロ＝ガラスの家」
1951年，リナ・ボ・バルディはブラジル市民となり，同年に最初に実現した建築＝夫妻の自邸である「カーザ・デ・ヴィドロ＝ガラスの家」を完成させた。この住宅は夫婦のためのプライベートな空間であるものの，同時に彼女がブラジルに残した大きな功績の記念碑的な始点であり，ブラジルで生涯を暮らすことになったこの家は，建築やデザインが個人やコミュニティ／社会，そして自然環境とどのような距離感を持つべきかを明瞭に示す最初の作品であり，この後彼女が手がけたすべての建築作品に，この最初の姿勢／精神が通底

After WWII, Brazilian architecture came to draw worldwide attention. But Brazilian architects such as Lúcio Costa, Oscar Niemeyer and Vilanova Artigas who studied European Modernism were not the only ones who contributed in driving their country's architectural environment into the future. One female architect/designer, Lina Bo Bardi, who has arrived from Italy after the war, was yet another of such key figures, as evidenced by current exhibitions and references relating to her. Instead of importing Modernist theories and historical traditional lineage of European architecture to Brazil, she introduced fundamental styles, theories and ideas of architecture that broke free from the rigidity of academism and expanded the realm of architecture. What she brought to Brazil was a way to discover and nurture beauty that enhances the society and everyday life in a generous, carefree manner. The spirit of the new culture and society that she presented traveled from the pre-colonial across the modern and contemporary times, threw the unique world of home-grown beauties that glimmered through each era into the limelight of her time, and tailored the present progressive architecture/design to convey an air of freedom, richness and fusion so typical of Brazil.

Lina Bo Bardi was born in Rome, Italy. After graduating from the College of Architecture at Rome University, she left for Milan and began her practice as an architect. But as design

work has proved to be scarce during wartime, she soon took up projects other than architecture, collaborating with the founding director of the magazine *Domus*, the architect/designer Giò Ponti, on a magazine, and drawing illustrations for other magazines and newspapers. After the war, she worked as a director at *Domus* for a year then returned to Rome and married the art critic/journalist Pietro Maria Bardi.

Eventually, the couple left the war-affected, stagnant Italy for a fresh new start in Brazil. First, Lina was offered a commission in Rio de Janeiro, then her husband Pietro was invited to establish and run the São Paulo Museum of Art (MASP, 1957-68). They decided to relocate to São Paulo where the couple spent the rest of their lives.

Casa de Vidro = The Glass House
In 1951, Lina Bo Bardi became a naturalized Brazilian citizen, and in the same year, completed her first real architectural project, the couple's home, Casa de Vidro (Glass House). This residence being a private space for the couple is also a monumental starting point of a series of achievements that she left in Brazil. This house that came to be their final home, was the first example that clearly demonstrated how architecture and design should keep a distance with individuals, community/society and natural environment: this initial stance/spirit would eventually underlie all of her subsequent architectural

していくこととなる。

それは建築に与えられる大きな許容性であり，堅苦しくない大らかな揺らぎである。コロニアルの伝統やそれ以前からあるフォークロアのプリミティブな美しさと，近現代の先進的な素材や技術が発するシャープさといった一見相反するような要素を混在させる大きな器としての建築である。そして建築とそこに起こるアクティビティは常に一体であり，整合性を超えた，生活を謳歌するヒューマニスティックな人生の舞台であった。

「ガラスの家」は，当時サンパウロ郊外であったモルンビー地区に残されたアトランティック・フォレストのジャングルの中に最初に建てられた住宅となった。約7千平米の広さの敷地は傾斜地であり，住宅はその頂き直前の傾斜面に建てられている。竣工当時の写真によれば，周囲のジャングルが今日までさらに深く育ってきたことは明らかであり，竣工当時の住宅内外部のモダニティに準じた簡潔な様子は，夫妻が50余年に育んできた様々な調度品や日常を飾るオブジェに埋め尽くされた今日の姿へ変貌したことと同期している。ヨーロッパから持ち込まれた近代は，ブラジルの地にローカライズされて新しい様相を獲得している。そもそもこの住宅はこの歳月の変化を全く拒むことなく成長することができるものであった。

道路より敷地に入ると，石畳は家に向かってカーブしながら登っていく。右手のガレージを通り過ぎ，石畳はその中央を陶器タイルの破片に飾られ直進した後，大きく左にカーブしていく。

そのカーブを曲がると住宅は深いジャングルの緑の中に現れる。細いスティールの円柱群によって支えられた，コンクリート・スラブと緩やかな傾斜の切妻屋根にサンドウィッチされたガラスのヴォリュームは，軽やかに緑の中に浮いている。石畳はさらに住宅下のピロティへと続いている。ピロティを支える青色の円柱は控えめなジェスチャーをする細さで，2本ずつ5列に立っている。周囲のジャングルの延長として土に覆われた地面から台座なしで立つ柱群は，あたかも木のごとく生えているかのようである。ピロティ上の薄いコンクリート・スラブには二つの方形の開口が与えられている。小さい方は上階玄関へと導く鉄製の階段のためのものであり，暗闇へと続いていくのに対して，大きい方は，建物を貫くヴォイドであり，陽光がここからは差し込んでいる。このヴォイドには彫刻的なシルエットの巨木が天に向かって伸び貫いており，この様は建物と周囲の自然との共生関係を象徴的に表明しているかのようである。

住宅はピロティに支えられる南東側主屋部分と，パティオによって距離の取られた北西側のサービス部分，そしてそれら二つの部分をつなぐパティオ

works.

It is about a greater tolerance afforded to architecture, an informal, benevolent fluctuation; it is about architecture as a large vessel to hold a mixture of apparently opposing elements such as the primitive beauty of the traditional Colonial and the even older Folkloric, and the sharpness of advanced materials and technologies of the modern and contemporary times. Architecture is always integral to activities that take place there. It is a humanistic stage of people's lives that transcends consistency and celebrates their everyday living.

The Glass House was the first residence to be built in the remnant jungle of the original Atlantic Forest in the neighborhood of Morumbi in the then suburbs of São Paulo. Boasting some 7,000 square meters of sloped terrain, the house sits near the crest of a hill. Looking at the photographs taken at the time of completion, it is apparent that the surrounding jungle has grown ever thicker, in synchronization with the concise aspect of the interior/exterior of the house at the time of its completion pursuant to Modernity turning into what it looks today, filled with a myriad of furnishings and items to adorn the daily life that the couple has amassed for over 50 years. The Modern that has been brought from Europe acquired new aspects by being localized to fit the land of Brazil. Right from the start, this residence was built to grow without ever refusing such

changes over the times.

As one enters the premises from the street, a winding paved path climbs up toward the house. Past the garage on the right, the path enters a straight line where it is decorated with fragments of ceramic tiles embedded in the center, then gently curves to the left.

After this curve, the house finally makes its appearance amid the thick green of the jungle. Supported on a set of spindly steel columns, the glazed volume sandwiched between a concrete slab and the gentle inclination of a gabled roof stays airily aloft against the green. The paved path continues to the pilotis underneath the house. Blue columns, whose slenderness keeps their gestures discreet, stand in pairs in 5 rows. Rising up directly from the earth-covered ground as an extension of the surrounding jungle with no foundation, these columns are reminiscent of a growth of trees. The thin concrete slab over the pilotis has two square-shaped openings: the smaller one accommodates a metal staircase leading up to the entrance toward the darkness, while the larger one is a void that pierces through the building from which sunlight pours down. In this void stands a giant tree with a sculpturesque silhouette stretching to the sky, as if expressing the symbiotic relationship between the building and the surrounding nature in a symbolic manner.

The house consists of the main wing on the southeast sup-

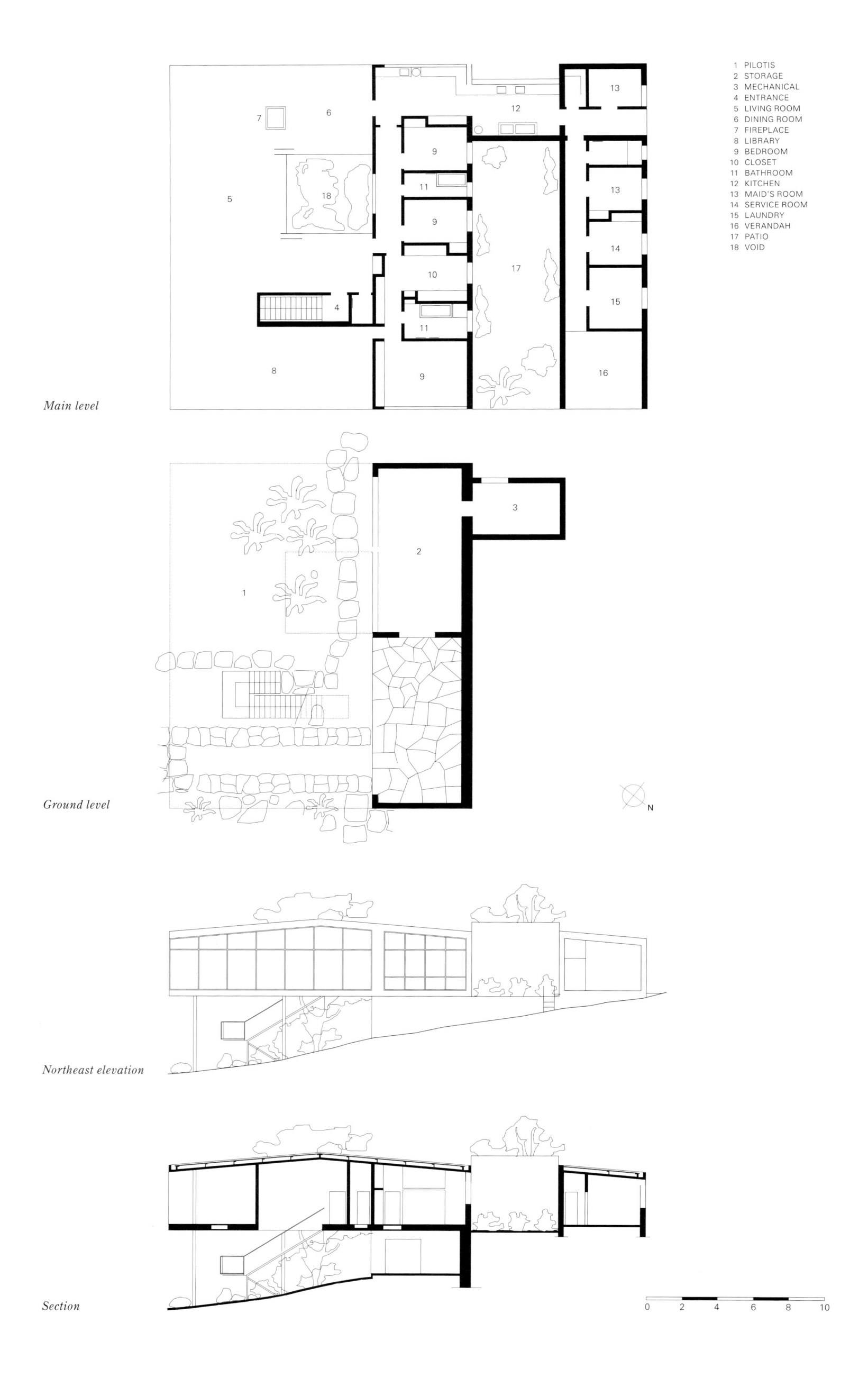

Main level

1 PILOTIS
2 STORAGE
3 MECHANICAL
4 ENTRANCE
5 LIVING ROOM
6 DINING ROOM
7 FIREPLACE
8 LIBRARY
9 BEDROOM
10 CLOSET
11 BATHROOM
12 KITCHEN
13 MAID'S ROOM
14 SERVICE ROOM
15 LAUNDRY
16 VERANDAH
17 PATIO
18 VOID

Ground level

Northeast elevation

Section

0 2 4 6 8 10

Approach. Garage on right, house on left behind woods

南西側の台所から構成されている。

　木製の踏み板とリベット留めされた鉄材による階段は，揺れることを前提としたように軽やかなシルエットを持ち，踊り場で方向を変えて暗い開口部に登っていく。しかし玄関を入ると明るく広々とした大空間に出る。居間，食堂，ライブラリーが緩やかにつながる大空間は，南東方向に下る敷地の斜面に向かって3方向に天井高のガラス壁が与えられ，周囲の緑と光を取り込んでいる。南半球ゆえに南側の開口は直接光を内部に取り込むためではなく，周囲の緑の光に照らされた様子を視覚的に取り込むものである。ガラス面にランダムに下がるカーテンのつくり出す光のリズムと背後に揺れる緑の気配は，絶えず変化して非均質で豊かな空間の様相をつくり，時の流れを演出している。緩やかに傾斜する白い大天井と，青いタイルの床と円柱群を共有している大空間は，様々な物であふれている。時代や出自，スタイル，趣味を超越した調度品や美術品，家具などが夫婦がここに暮らした豊かな痕跡としてすべて空間の一部となっている。存在感のある家具や様々なラグは，基本的にはモダニズムの理念に根ざすこの空間を緩やかに分節して，差異のある場面の連続体としている。

　前述のヴォイド，ピロティから天に向かって伸びる1本の木の姿は居間と食堂の両方からそれぞれのガラス壁を通して見ることができ，また90度に折れたこれら2枚のガラス壁を通して，居間と食堂は直接的ではなく見通せる関係性がつくられている。同様に，自立している暖炉は居間と食堂を緩やかに分ける役割を果たしている。

　玄関と階段室を囲う白壁によってライブラリーはややプライベートな性格が与えられているが，南東側では居間を見通している。多くの本を収めたスティール書架やファイル・キャビネットが置かれたライブラリーの北西側の奥にはさらにプライベートな主寝室が配置されている。主寝室は北東側に開口を持ち，朝陽を導いている。

　主寝室の南西側に配置された二つの小寝室は北西側のパティオに向かって開口部を持ち，サービス部分の白い壁面を見ることになる。

　台所は居間，食堂のタイルと異なり，黒色タイルの床，緑色とクリーム色を基調とした壁を持つ空間で，食堂とサービス部分の間にあって機能的なアクセスを獲得している。

　使用人の住居となるサービス部分は斜面の上段に位置する一層のヴォリュームで，主屋と明快に分離されている。

リナ・ボ・バルデイはこの名作住宅を完成させた後，数は少ないがブラジル建築界におけるマイル・ストーンとなる作品を完成させる。「サンパウロ美術

ported on the pilotis, the service area on the northwest kept at a distance across the patio, and the kitchen that bridges the two on the southwestern side of the patio.

Composed of wooden treads and riveted metal members, the staircase has a weightless silhouette as if it were conceived on the assumption that it will sway, makes a turn at the landing and climbs up to the dark opening. But once inside the entrance, a vast light-filled space awaits: housing the living room, the dining room and the library that are loosely connected with each other, the vast open space features floor-to-ceiling glass walls on three sides looking down the sloping site toward southeast that introduce natural light and the view of surrounding green. Being in the southern hemisphere, openings on the south are not meant to introduce light to the inside in a direct manner, but to introduce a view of the surrounding green being illuminated by sunlight. The rhythm of light generated by curtains hung randomly on the glass surfaces and hints of green that sways behind constantly change as they create rich and heterogeneous aspects of the space as well as orchestrate the flow of time. This vast space that shares a gently inclined white ceiling, blue tiled floor and a set of columns is overflowing with various objects: furnishings and art collections that transcend time, history, styles and tastes are all integrated to become part of the space as a rich trace left by the couple who lived there. Various rugs and pieces of furniture with powerful presence loosely segmentalize this space which is essentially rooted in Modernism and turn it into a continuum of distinct scenes.

The image of a single tree stretching from the aforementioned void, the pilotis, to the sky can be seen from both the living room and the dining room, through the glazed walls in each room. Also, through these two sets of glazed walls that each forms a 90-degree angle, an indirect visibility is established between the living and dining rooms. At the same time, the freestanding fireplace plays a function in loosely separating these two rooms.

White walls that enclose the entrance and the stair hall account for the library's private character, despite the fact that visibility of the living room is ensured on the southeastern side. Further back on the northwestern side of the library that accommodates file cabinets and steel shelves full of books is the master bedroom that provides even more privacy; it has an opening on northeast to let the morning sunshine in.

Two small bedrooms arranged on the southwest of the master bedroom feature openings facing the patio on the northwest but with a view of white walls of the service area.

The kitchen is a space with black tiled floor, unlike those in living and dining rooms, and walls in green and cream hues, and provides a functional access between the dining room and the service area.

館（MASP）」や「SESC ポンペイア文化スポーツセンター」(1977-86年)といった
ブラジル建築界に大きな影響を与えた作品である。いずれの作品も「ガラス
の家」を起点としたブラジルとの「付き合い方」をさらに革新的に展開してい
る。

　「サンパウロ美術館」での，大胆な構造形態と判りやすい赤色のフレーム
がつくる都市のイコンとしての強いメッセージ，そして実際に足元につくり出
されたパブリックスペースは，サンパウロ市の市民と訪問者両方にとって，世
界唯一と言えるほどの大名所であり，今日まで親しまれ続けている。建築的
な視点ではやや単純で大胆な美術館は，都市の中に置かれた親しみやすい
「家具」であり，常識的スケールを超越したその勇姿はブラジルの大衆へ強
く発信するものであった。

　「SESC ポンペイア文化スポーツセンター」の増改築においても，既存の工
場空間を最大級に残し，判りやすいヴォキャブラリーで強度のあるプリミ
ティブなデザインを与えることで，一過性ではない永続的な大衆の要請に答
えた施設に仕立てた。

リナ・ボ・バルディの建築を考えるとき，モダニズムの女性建築家／デザイ
ナーである二人が思い出される。一人はアイリーン・グレイであり，もう一人
はシャルロット・ペリアンである。

　三人に共通するのは，フェミニンで優しく細やかなデザインの感性と，そ
れを実現して前に進んでいく強靭なバイタリティの両方を持った才能であっ
たこと，建築の領域を大衆化するような判りやすく永続的なデザインを残し
たことである。

　20世紀は男社会の建築界において女性作家の特質が際立ち台頭していく
時代の幕開けであった。リナ・ボ・バルディも女性作家として時代の要請に
見事に応え，新しい社会性に答える建築／デザインのプロトタイプを残した
のだった。

The service area housing the servants' apartments is a single-layer volume located at the top of the slope, clearly separated from the main wing.

Following the completion of this residential masterpiece, Lina Bo Bardi created a handful of milestones of Brazilian architecture such as the São Paulo Museum of Art (MASP) and the SESC Pompéia (culture and sports center, 1977-86) that exerted a major influence on the architectural world in Brazil. Each of these works represents an innovative development of the "way of interacting with" Brazil, that originated with her Glass House.

The São Paulo Museum of Art's powerful message as an urban icon produced by the audacious structural form and an easily comprehensible red frame, together with the public space created beneath it became, for both the citizens of São Paulo and the visitors, one of the world's most unique landmark, and enjoys an ongoing popularity. Fairly simple and bold from an architectural perspective, the museum is an accessible "furniture" placed in a city. Its brave figure that surpasses the common-sense scale delivered a powerful appeal to the Brazilian public.

The renovation/extension work for the SESC Pompéia also consisted of keeping the maximum of the existing factory space and providing an intense primitive design using comprehensible vocabulary in order to create a facility that responded to the public needs that were lasting rather than transient.

As I think about Lina Bo Bardi's architecture, two female Modernist architects/designers come to my mind. One is Eileen Gray; the other is Charlotte Perriand.

What these three women had in common were their talent equipped with both a feminine, gentle and delicate design sensitivity and a strong and tough vitality to materialize such sensitivity and move forward, and their achievements in the creation of easy-to-understand, lasting designs that would popularize the realm of architecture.

The 20th century saw the dawning of an age when the characteristics of female artists began to stand out and come to the forefront of the architectural world, which has long been a man's world. And Lina Bo Bardi as a female artist succeeded in meeting the needs of the times and achieved prototypes of architecture/design that responded to a new type of society.

English translation by Lisa Tani

Approach: pieces of ceramic tile are embeded

View toward approach from entrance staircase

Approach and house. House sitting on steep hillside, covered with woods, and gate on left

Overall view from east

Entrance staircase

Void for tree: looking southwest. Dining room above

Pilotis with thin columns of 17 cm in diameter

Pilotis: looking southeast

Southwest elevation with kitchen window

View from west: rear entrance for service rooms

Pilotis

Void: looking northeast

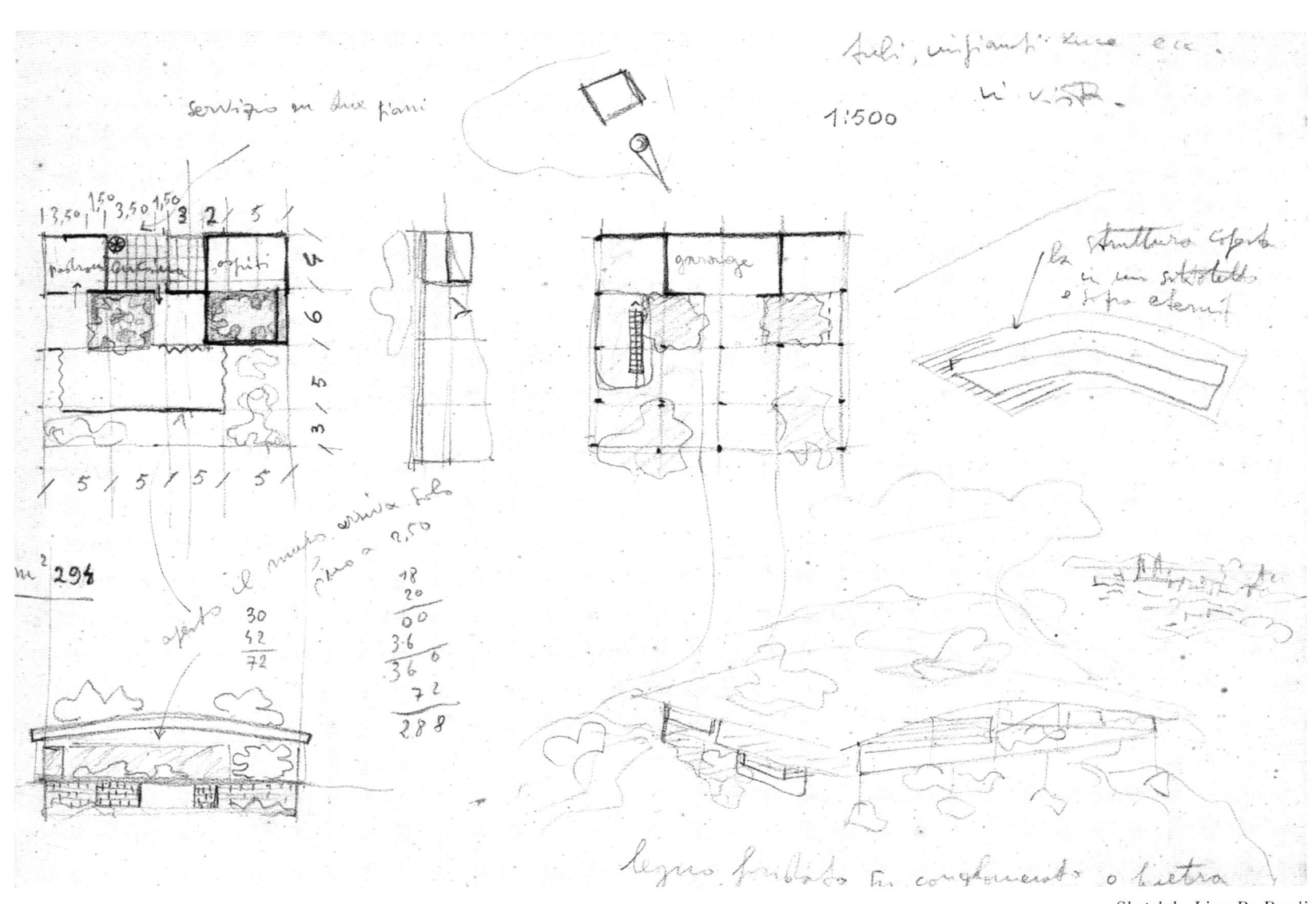

Sketch by Lina Bo Bardi

Entrance staircase: steel structure with wooden steps

30

Entrance staircase

Downward view from entrance

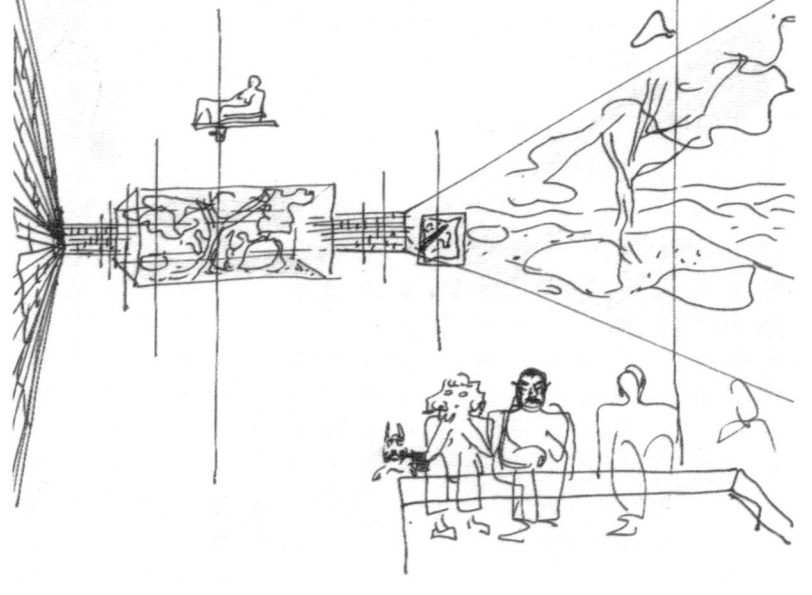

Sketches by Lina Bo Bardi

View from staircase toward entrance

Entrance door

Living room

Living room: looking southwest

Living room: looking southeast

Living room: opening on southwest

Living room: view toward library

Fireplace at living room. Dining room behind

40

View toward dining room through void above pilotis

View from entrance toward living room

Entrance on left, library on right. Lounge table

Library

Library : north corner

Library : east corner

Table with furnishings at livng room

Dining room

View from dining room toward living room through void above pilotis

Dining room: view toward door to kitchen

Kitchen: view toward dining room

Kitchen

Bedroom

Window at bedroom

Corridor: window facing void above pilotis

世界現代住宅全集 22
リナ・ボ・バルディ
カーザ・デ・ヴィドロ（ガラスの家）

2016 年 7 月 25 日発行
文・編集：二川由夫
撮影：二川幸夫
アート・ディレクション：細谷巌

印刷・製本：大日本印刷株式会社
制作・発行：エーディーエー・エディタ・トーキョー
151-0051　東京都渋谷区千駄ヶ谷 3-12-14
TEL.（03）3403-1581（代）

禁無断転載

ISBN 978-4-87140-647-5 C1352